What a Home!

Melissa Blackwell Burke and Chris Jaeggi

sundance™

A Haights Cross Communications Company

Published by
Sundance Publishing
P.O. Box 740
One Beeman Road
Northborough, MA 01532-0740
800-343-8204
www.sundancepub.com

Illustrations by Kevin Rechin

Photo Credits
Cover (top) Stuart Westmorland/Corbis; Cover (bottom) Joseph Sohm/ChromoSohm
Inc./Corbis; p. 1 Royalty-free/Corbis; p. 6 Franck Fotos/Alamy; p. 8 Dan Ferguson; p. 9
Dan Ferguson; p. 10 (bottom) Katherine Stanczak; p. 10 (top right) stock.xchng;
p. 11 (top) HGTV/Extreme Homes of Exotic Islands; p. 11 (center) Joseph Sohm/
ChromoSohm Inc./Corbis; pp. 14–15 Hans Strand/Corbis; p. 15 Michael Freeman/
Corbis; pp. 16–17 (top) Torsten Blackwood/AFP/Getty Images; pp. 16–17 (bottom)
James Pozarik/Getty Images; pp. 18–19 Lindsay Hebberd/Corbis; p. 22 adrian arbib/
Alamy; p. 23 Peter Adams Photography/Alamy; pp. 24–25 Peter Adams Photography/
Alamy; p. 26 (inset) WaterwayHouseboats; p. 26 (bottom) Royalty-Free/Corbis; p. 27
Courtesy Plane Boats, Inc.; pp. 28–29 (top) Digital Vision/Getty Images; pp. 28–29
(center) Alan Levenson/Stone/Getty Images; Back cover (left) Dan Ferguson; Back
cover (right) Katherine Stanczak

ISBN–13: 978-1-4207-0326-9
ISBN–10: 1-4207-0326-9

Printed in China

TABLE OF CONTENTS

Home, Strange Home

Is it a shoe? Is it a shell? Is it a UFO?

No. It's none of those things. It's a house built in a shape that surprises people.

Let's visit some houses that are not your average rectangle shape. What would you think if these homes were next door?

And a Home to Boot!

"There was an old woman who lived in a shoe." But wait. Have you heard about the home shaped like a boot?

I love to heel!

Colonel Mahlon Haines owned more than 40 shoe stores. So he built the Shoe House to **advertise** his business. Even the doghouse is in the shape of a boot.

Haines let some people stay in the house. A maid and butler waited on them. And they got free shoes! Today, people can tour the house. Tourists may even get a snack called "Heelbasi" in the snack bar in the heel.

Q: What kind of dress does a house wear?
A: An address!

Ship Shape

What's that **perched** on a hill near Denver, Colorado? It looks like a spaceship or a flying saucer! But don't call the police.

The Sculptured House

A big living space

The house is called the Sculptured House,
and it doesn't fly. It is set in the ground on
steel posts. The outside is a concrete shell.

Inside, you can walk up a circular staircase.
Or you can take an elevator shaped like a
tube. Just don't get lost in the more than
7,000 square feet of living space!

Shelter in a Shell

An alarm clock buzzes. A toilet flushes. The sounds are coming from a giant **conch** shell. How can that be? It can happen if the shell is someone's home.

On the outside, there's no mistaking the shell shape. Even the windows look like holes you might see in a real shell.

The shell house

My dream house!

This house, located on an island near Cancun, Mexico, is easy to find. Look for the biggest conch shell you've ever seen.

Shell faucet handles

Dome, Sweet Dome

More than 50 years ago, R. Buckminster Fuller came up with the idea of the dome home. It is strong enough to withstand high winds and costs less to heat and cool. And you can have the only house on the block that looks sort of like a soccer ball! **11**

Climate Control

Snow houses in Florida—no way!
Grass roofs in the Arctic—BRRRR!

The kind of house you build really depends on the **climate**. People usually build homes that are best for the climate they live in. Grab your sweater and flip-flops, and let's find out how climate and **shelter** go together!

Chilling Out!

Want to get away to a cool spot? You can chill out at the Ice Hotel in Quebec, Canada. It's made of 12,000 tons of snow and 400 tons of ice. Even the furniture is ice.

Every year there is a new Ice Hotel. Why? Because when spring arrives, it's bye-bye, ice and snow!

Inside the Ice Hotel

Dining on ice

Snow Wonder

Igloos can be built in one to two hours out of shaped blocks of snow. And snow actually keeps the inside of the igloo warm enough for a family to be comfortable.

Can You Dig It?

Do deep, dark basements give you the creeps? Imagine what it would be like if your whole house were underground.

I could really use a window.

A bedroom down under

People in an Australian town decided to make underground homes called **dugouts.** Some of the dugouts are old mine shafts. These homes are cool in summer and warm in winter.

Thatch Is Where It's At

Grass on a roof? You bet! A grass called alang-alang makes a great roof in warm, tropical climates. It's a type of **thatched** roof, which is made of plant materials.

Alang-alang has to be completely dried out. Then it's tied to bamboo to make a roof that can last as long as 20 years. It protects the home from heat and cold, and it keeps rain out. Now that is some tough grass!

Alang-alang roofs in Southeast Asia

19

On the Move

Zoom! Zoom! Do you like to travel but miss home when you're away?

Who says you can't have both? Let's see how you can be at home and away at the same time in these homes on the move.

But where are its legs?

Ger-r-reat!

Grab your backpack and hiking boots, but leave your tent at home. You'll be staying in a ger.

Inside a traditional ger

A ger—also called a yurt—is a tentlike home in Mongolia. It has a wooden frame covered with large pieces of felt. Gers can be packed up and moved around. This is important because the people who live in them have to move their herds to find food and water.

Do It
Yurt-Self
Moving

Hairy Tents

The Bedouins make wool from goat and camel hair. They use this woven wool to make their tents because it is warm and it keeps out water.

If you don't get up, Frank, I'm going to make a tent out of you!

Look behind you, Fred. They already did!

Bedouin camp

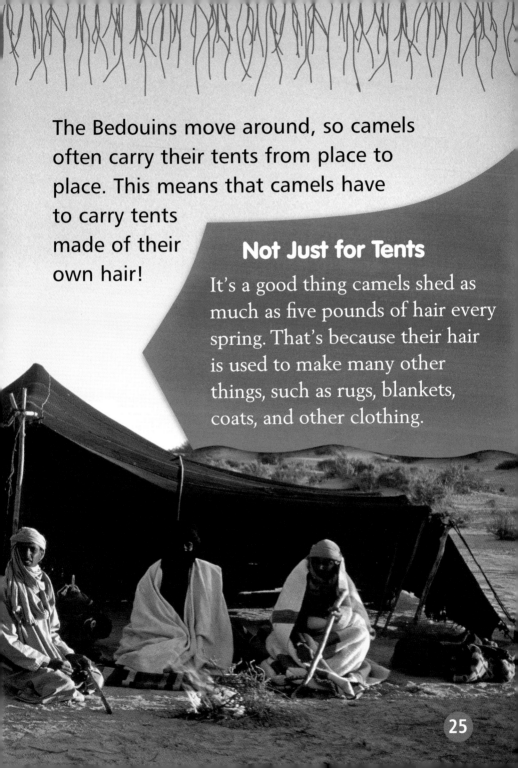

The Bedouins move around, so camels often carry their tents from place to place. This means that camels have to carry tents made of their own hair!

Not Just for Tents

It's a good thing camels shed as much as five pounds of hair every spring. That's because their hair is used to make many other things, such as rugs, blankets, coats, and other clothing.

At Home on the Water

Houseboats are homes on the water. Some of them are on the move, and others stay in one place. Their owners have no lawns to mow. In fact, they may be able to lean out a window and catch fish for dinner.

"Backyard" slide

15 Water Street. This must be the place!

Houseboats come in all shapes and sizes. Rolling down the river in a houseboat sounds like fun—if you don't get seasick!

Whatever Floats Your Boat

It's a plane. It's a boat. It's both! This floating plane has been stripped of its wings and tail and changed into a houseboat called the Cosmic Muffin. Once a high-flying plane, it's now one of the most streamlined houseboats you'll ever see. This 56-foot boat still has its original airplane seats. All of the controls are in the cockpit. Come aboard!

Taking It on the Road

Go to sleep in Texas and wake up in Florida? If you're traveling in a motor home, you can. Some people are on the road in their motor homes all the time. Others use them for vacations. For camping or full-time living, motor homes are the speediest of all houses.

What kind of house will **YOU** call home?

Fact File

You might say that Colonel Haines, the man who built the Shoe House, wanted to be recognized. He would stand up at baseball games and offer money to anyone who knew who he was!

April warmth melts Canada's Ice Hotel, but a new one is built in about five weeks the next winter. So the design of the hotel—including new ice sculptures—changes each year!

Some of the underground dugout homes in Australia began as opal mines. One man who carved out a 17-room home found enough of these gems to pay for his entire home!

Glossary

advertise to let others know about something

climate average weather conditions in a place

conch a large, spiral-shaped shell

dugouts shelters dug in a hillside or underground

perched sitting in a high place

shelter a place that covers and protects

thatched covered with plant material that is used for roofing

Index